More Parables of Jesus

By

B. A. Ramsbottom

2013

GOSPEL STANDARD TRUST PUBLICATIONS
12(b) Roundwood Lane
Harpenden, Herts, AL5 3BZ
England

Published by:
Gospel Standard Trust Publications

1989
Reprinted 1993
Reset and reprinted 2013

ISBN: 978 0 903556 81 1

Printed by:
Hung Hing Offset Printing Co. Ltd.
China

The Foolish Farmer

Have you ever been out into the fields when it is harvest time? Whichever way you look you can see the lovely golden corn growing. It is a beautiful sight.

There was once a farmer who had many fields of corn. Wherever he looked he could see his corn growing, ripening for harvest. He was a very rich man.

But he was worried. He just did not know where he would keep all his corn when it was gathered in at harvest time. He had not nearly enough room.

So he began to think. And then he had a good idea. He would pull down all his little barns, which were too small, and build really big ones instead.

That was a good idea, wasn't it? Well, the rich farmer thought so!

Then he thought of what a good time he would have. Plenty of money. Plenty to eat and drink. A merry life!

But do you know what happened? The very day he was thinking these things, he died. And what of all his corn, and his fields, and his money, and his barns? Somebody else would have them.

Jesus said what a foolish man the rich farmer was. He was getting ready to do all sorts of things – but he was not ready to die! He never thought about God.

Jesus spoke a solemn word: "What shall it profit a man, if he shall gain the whole world, and lose his own soul?"

You can read this story in Luke chapter 12, verses 16 to 21.

There is a little prayer. May God teach you to pray it:

Prepare me, gracious God,
　To stand before Thy face;
Thy Spirit must the work perform,
　For it is all of grace.

The Lost Coin

One day a woman sat sadly in her house. She had lost a silver coin. It was worth a lot. No wonder she was sad.

Perhaps some of you girls and boys have lost something you really like – and how you long to find it! You cannot be happy till you do.

Now altogether this woman should have had ten silver pieces – so she still had nine left. Her friends might have said to her, "Stop worrying! You still have plenty left!"

But no! How could she? She knew that her lost coin must be somewhere. So she started to search the house for it.

Houses in Bible times were always dark, which made it harder for her. Also the floors were usually covered with rushes (like we have a carpet). So she lit a candle to help her to see, and she took up a broom to sweep through the house.

She kept at it. She would not give up. And at last – there it was! Her lost coin!

She was so pleased that she ran out of her house and told all her friends and those who lived nearby. She said, "I have found the piece of money which I had lost."

Girls and boys, we too are LOST – lost through our sin. And we need the Lord Jesus to seek us out and find us.

Did you know that He once said, "The Son of Man is come to seek and to save that which was lost"? That is why He came from heaven to earth to die. And how pleased He is when He finds those He came to save!

You can read this parable in Luke chapter 15, verses 8 to 10.

The Wedding Garment

I wonder how many of you have ever been asked to a wedding. If you have, then there is one thing I know you did. You wore your best clothes. Perhaps you even had a new suit or a new dress for the wedding. Afterwards there was a lovely meal.

The Lord Jesus once spoke about a very special wedding. It was the wedding of a prince. All sorts of people were invited — but they made sure that for such a wonderful occasion they were wearing wedding clothes. Only the very best!

Afterwards there was the lovely meal. It *would* be lovely (wouldn't it?) if it was made ready by the king. We do not know everything that they had to eat, but we are told one thing. They had roast ox!

And then the time they were waiting for arrived. The king himself came in. He walked round to see the guests.

But what is happening now? The king has stopped going round. He seems angry. He is talking to one man.

Well, it is no wonder that the king is angry. Look what the man is wearing! Just his ordinary clothes. He is different from all the others who are there. Did you ever see a person at a wedding in old clothes? And this was a royal wedding.

Now, it was not that the man was so poor that he

had no wedding clothes, and couldn't afford to buy any. Don't think that! At a royal wedding in Bible times a lovely wedding garment would be provided free of charge. But this man didn't want one! He thought his own clothes were quite good enough.

At last the king speaks. He asks him what he is doing there, dressed as he is. It is an insult to the king, the prince, and to everyone else.

And, do you know, the man could not answer a word. He just did not know what to say. He was speechless.

But then the king spoke again, and told his servants to take the man, and to throw him out. He was not allowed to stay there a moment longer.

How important it is that we do not trust in anything of our own before God, anything we are or have done! Our very best, in God's sight, is just like a bundle of dirty rags. We need to be washed in the blood of Jesus and the spotless robe of His righteousness put upon us.

You can read this parable in Matthew chapter 22, verses 11 to 14.

The Pharisee and the Publican

In Jerusalem there was a beautiful, big temple. The Jews loved it. It was such a lovely building, and it was there that they worshipped the great God, who made heaven and earth.

Jesus told us of two men inside that beautiful temple. Both of them had gone there to pray to God. But look at them! What a difference!

One of them is standing there very boldly. What a fine man he is, and how proud! Everyone admires him. He is wearing a long dress with tassels and a fringe at the bottom, and a golden tablet on his forehead. He is a Pharisee.

But now look at the other! He seems afraid. He is standing out of sight in a corner. He is looking at the ground. No one likes him. He is a tax collector or publican (and usually they were greedy and not honest).

Now listen to the Pharisee praying. What a wonderful man he is! He tells God all the good things he has been doing – giving money away, never acting wrongly. But wait a moment! We do not hear him asking for anything. It seems that there is nothing he wants God to do for him. And doesn't he talk unkindly about the publican?

How different the poor man in the corner! But what is he doing? He is beating on his chest, just

where his heart is. He feels so troubled inside.

But at last he speaks – and what a short, simple, beautiful prayer: "God be merciful to me a sinner!"

He knew God is holy and good. He felt that he himself was wicked and bad. If only this great God would forgive him! So he cried out for mercy. He didn't deserve it – but perhaps God would show pity on him.

He would know that in this wonderful temple there used to be a place called "the mercy seat." It was precious, made of pure gold, and once a year blood was sprinkled on it. And he knew God had promised to meet His people there.

Would God be like that mercy seat to him?

> "Mercy, through blood, I make my plea;
> O God, be merciful to me."

Now hear the Lord Jesus Himself speak. He said that when the poor publican went home that day, he was the one that God loved and had forgiven. One day he would go to heaven.

Girls and boys, may God teach you each to pray the publican's prayer: "GOD BE MERCIFUL TO ME A SINNER."

You can read this parable in Luke chapter 18, verses 9 to 14.

The Tares in the Cornfield

There was once a farmer who wanted to have a really good harvest. So he made sure that all the seed he sowed was good. He thought: "If it is good seed, then it will grow up into good corn." He thought of the time when his field would be full of golden corn.

But who is that man, and what is he doing? It is dark, and everyone is asleep. There he is wandering round the cornfield. Do you know what he is doing? How sad! He is sowing bad weeds.

The Bible tells us why. It was because he did not like the farmer. He wanted to do him harm. It was a very unkind thing to do.

The weeds he sowed were called "tares." When they begin to grow, they look just like the good corn. You cannot tell any difference. But when the harvest comes, it can be seen they are only weeds. There is no good grain in the tares to be made into bread.

But some of the workmen on the farm began to realise what had happened. "Master," they said, "let us go round and pull them all up!"

"No!" said their master. "They look so much like the good wheat that you will pull some of that up as well. At harvest time we will sort them out."

There are some people everyone thinks are real Christians. They look just like them – but really they are not. They are like those weeds, the tares, not the wheat.

But at last it was harvest and the farmer gathered out all the tares – and what did he do with them? He burned them. The good wheat was gathered safely into his barn.

At the end of the world those people who are like the tares will be cast out to be burned. God will be able to tell the difference. But those like the good corn will be gathered safely into heaven.

God's people are no better than others – but God makes them different. Their sins are all washed away in the blood of Jesus. They will be safely gathered into heaven at last.

You can read this parable in Matthew chapter 13, verses 24 to 30 and verses 36 to 43.

We sometimes sing these verses at harvest time:

> All the world is God's own field,
> Fruit unto His praise to yield;
> Wheat and tares together sown,
> Unto joy or sorrow grown;
> First the blade, and then the ear,
> Then the full corn shall appear;
> Lord of harvest, grant that we
> Wholesome grain and pure may be.

For the Lord our God shall come,
And shall take His harvest home;
From His field shall in that day
All offences purge away;
Give His angels charge at last
In the fire the tares to cast;
But the fruitful ears to store
In His garner evermore.

The Fishing Net

Have you ever been fishing? Or have you been at the seaside and seen the fishing boats going out to sea? Later they come back, laden with fish – and often there are lots of seagulls, hovering round and screaming, trying to get some of the fish for themselves.

In Bible days, the fishermen took a large fishing net out to sea and caught the fish that swam into it. Sometimes they had to wait a long time till the net was filled. Then when it was full, they pulled it back to the shore.

The Lord Jesus tells us what they did before they sold the fish. They went carefully through all that they had caught. Some of the fish they could sell; they were good to eat. But some were no use; no one would buy them; they were just not fit to eat.

So what did the fishermen do? They gathered the good fish into their baskets, but the bad fish they threw away.

Jesus said: At the end of the world the angels will do what the fishermen were doing. They will gather all God's people safely into heaven, but will throw the wicked into a terrible fire.

All the fish had been in the same net; but it will do us no good if we have only been at Sunday school or chapel with God's people. If we are not made real Christians, we shall be cast out – for ever.

You can read this parable in Matthew chapter 13, verses 47 to 50.

A little hymn:
> Pause, my soul, and ask the question,
> > Am I ready to meet God?
> Am I made a real Christian,
> > Washed in the Redeemer's blood?

The Wicked Workmen

So many of the stories the Lord Jesus told were about farmers.

This one did not grow corn, or keep cows and pigs, but he grew grapes. He planted some vines – the trees on which grapes grow. Then he put a hedge all the way round so that no one could steal his grapes or any wild animals get at them. After that he made a winepress – a place where the juice could be squeezed out of the grapes to make wine. He would be able to sell the wine for a lot of money. Last of all he built a high tower so that everything could be carefully watched and no harm would come to his vines.

When everything was finished, he went far away to another country. But what about his lovely vineyard?

Well, he got a lot of men to look after it for him. He would pay them, but all the grapes and the wine would be his.

At last the time came. His lovely vineyard was full of ripe grapes. So he sent his servants to bring all the fruit to him. But do you know what the wicked workmen who were looking after the vineyard did? They threw stones at one of the servants. Another they beat with sticks. And one they even killed.

So the farmer sent some more of his servants. He wanted the grapes from his vines, or the wine that was made, or at least the money. But the workmen looking after the vineyard did just the same thing. They attacked them. They wanted to keep everything for themselves.

At last the farmer had an idea. He thought, "I will send my own son. Surely they will listen to him."

But no! The cruel workmen waited for him, and then jumped on him and killed him. They said, "Now everything is ours!"

When Jesus had told this sad story, He asked a question — and we all know the answer. He said, "What do you think the farmer will do?"

All those listening cried, "He will punish those wicked workmen, and he will find others to look after his vineyard instead." They knew what a dreadful thing the men had done.

And then Jesus shocked them. He told them that they were just like the wicked men. They would not listen to God's prophets and teachers, and at last they would crucify His Son.

How we need God to make us sorry for our sins and to ask His forgiveness! And how thankful we should be that God sent His own Son, the Lord Jesus, to die for sinners!

You can read this story in Matthew 21, verses 33-44; Mark 12, verses 1-12; and Luke 20, verses 9-18.

The Hidden Treasure

One day a man was digging in a field. Suddenly his spade struck something. What was it?

Carefully he looked. To his amazement he saw gold, silver, precious stones. It was treasure he had found.

So what did he do? He did not steal it. He did not even take part of it home. He carefully covered it up so that no one could see it – and then went home.

Often in Bible days people would hide things in the ground. There was nothing else they could do, was there? To keep something safe, which they specially valued, they would dig a hole in the ground and hide it there. Sometimes they died without telling anyone about it.

But what was the man going to do who had found this treasure? He was so thrilled with what he had found. He wanted it so badly. So he did what he was allowed to do. He thought, "I will buy the whole field; then the treasure will be mine."

But no! he had not enough money. When he counted up all that he had, it was not enough. But he did want that hidden treasure!

So he sold all that he had – *everything*. And then quickly, gladly, he went and paid the money – and the field was his.

Now he had that treasure. No one could take it

from him. And he was so happy. It was worth giving everything else up.

The Lord Jesus is the most precious thing in this world. He is the greatest treasure. May God make us willing to part with everything if only we might have Jesus for our Saviour and Friend.

You can read this parable in Matthew chapter 13, verse 44.